the SCIENCE beHIND
ANIMAL AND PLANT SURVIVAL

Nicolas Brasch

- ➲ What Happens When a Food Chain Breaks?

- ➲ What Does "Survival of the Fittest" Mean?

- ➲ If Cheetahs Are One of the Fastest Animals on Earth, Why Are They Endangered?

This edition first published in 2011 in the United States of America by Smart Apple Media. All rights reserved. No part of this book may be reproduced in any form or by any means without written permission from the publisher.

Smart Apple Media
P.O. Box 3263
Mankato, MN, 56002

First published in 2010 by
MACMILLAN EDUCATION AUSTRALIA PTY LTD
15–19 Claremont St, South Yarra, Australia 3141

Visit our web site at www.macmillan.com.au or go directly to www.macmillanlibrary.com.au

Associated companies and representatives throughout the world.

Copyright © Nicolas Brasch 2010

Library of Congress Cataloging-in-Publication Data

Brasch, Nicolas.
    Animal and plant survival / Nicolas Brasch.
        p. cm. — (The science behind)
    Includes index.
    ISBN 978-1-59920-559-5 (library binding)
    1. Animals—Adaptation—Juvenile literature. 2. Plants—Adaptation—Juvenile literature.
    3. Adaptation (Biology)—Juvenile literature. I. Title.
    QH546.B74 2011
    578.4—dc22

                                                                    2009045105

Publisher: Carmel Heron
Managing Editor: Vanessa Lanaway
Editor: Georgina Garner
Proofreader: Kylie Cockle
Designer: Stella Vassiliou
Page layout: Stella Vassiliou and Raul Diche
Photo researcher: Sarah Johnson
Illustrators: Alan Laver, pp. 7, 14, 16, 18, 22, 23, 25; Richard Morden, pp. 17, 26; Karen Young p. 1.
Production Controller: Vanessa Johnson

Manufactured in China by Macmillan Production (Asia) Ltd.
Kwun Tong, Kowloon, Hong Kong
Supplier Code: CP December 2009

Acknowledgments
The author and the publisher are grateful to the following for permission to reproduce copyright material:

Front cover photographs:
Fly caught in Venus fly Trap (Dionaea muscipula), Clive Nichols/Getty Images; Chameleon, © mashe/Shutterstock; Grizzly bear fishing for salmon, © oksana.perkins/Shutterstock.

Photos courtesy of:
© Muller Fred-Biosphoto/AUSCAPE. All rights reserved, **12** (left); © Reg Morrison/AUSCAPE. All rights reserved, **12** (top); James Balog/Getty Images, **31** (bottom right); David Burder/Getty Images, **14**; Peter David/Getty Images, **11**; Ken & Michelle Dyball/ Getty Images, **6** (bottom); FPG/Getty Images, **18** (top right); National Geographic/Getty Images, **30**; Norbert Rosing/Getty Images, **23**; © John Bayliss/iStockphoto, **18** (bottom); © Peter Garbet/iStockphoto, **15** (right); © Cathy Keifer/iStockphoto, **9**; © Sven Klaschik/iStockphoto, **4**; © Johan Swanepoel/iStockphoto, **20** (top); Kennedy Space Center of the United States National Aeronautics and Space Administration (NASA), **31** (top); Clive Bromhall/Photolibrary, **31** (middle right); Paroli Galperti/Photolibrary, **24** (right); Tim Jackson/Photolibrary, **13** (bottom); Breck P Kent/Photolibrary, **19**; Wayne Lynch/Photolibrary, **28**; Tom McHugh/ Photolibrary, **31** (middle left); Oxford Scientific/Photolibrary, **15** (left); HS. Terrace/Photolibrary, **31** (bottom left); John Warburton-Lee Photography/Photolibrary, **7**; Dr Ken MacDonald/Science Photo Library, **10**; © Stephane Angue/Shutterstock, **20** (bottom); © Paul Banton/Shutterstock, **5**; © FloridaStock/Shutterstock, **27**; © Steffen Foerster Photography/Shutterstock, **21**; © Leighton Photography & Imaging/Shutterstock, **24** (left); © Steve Lovegrove/Shutterstock, **12** (bottom); © mashe/Shutterstock, **8**; © Christian Musat/Shutterstock, **13** (top); © oksana.perkins/Shutterstock, **29**.

List sourced from Irving Wallace, David Wallechinsky and Amy Wallace, The Book of Lists 2, Bantam, 1980, **31**.

While every care has been taken to trace and acknowledge copyright, the publisher tenders their apologies for any accidental infringement where copyright has proved untraceable. Where the attempt has been unsuccessful, the publisher welcomes information that would redress the situation.

The publisher would like to thank Heidi Ruhnau, Head of Science at Oxley College, for her assistance in reviewing manuscripts.

Please note
At the time of printing, the Internet addresses appearing in this book were correct. Owing to the dynamic nature of the Internet, however, we cannot guarantee that all these addresses will remain correct.

▶ Contents

Look out for these features throughout the book:

"Word Watch" explains the meanings of
words shown in **bold**

"Web Watch" provides web site
suggestions for further research

Understanding the World Through Science

Science = Knowledge
The word "science" comes from the Latin word *scientia*, which means "knowledge."

W ord Watch

experimentation using scientific procedures to make discoveries, test ideas, and prove facts

observation watching carefully in order to gain information

▲ Humans look at the things around them and ask "Why?" and "How?" Science helps answer these questions.

Science is amazing! Through science, people can understand more about the world and themselves. Without science, humans would not have a clue—about anything!

Shared Knowledge

Science exists because humans are curious. They are curious about how things work, about Earth and its place in the universe, about life and survival, about the natural world around them, and about time, space, and speed. They are curious about everything! They never stop asking questions.

Science is the knowledge that humans have gathered about the physical and natural world and how it works. This knowledge is gathered through **experimentation** and **observation**.

The Science Behind Animal and Plant Survival

Humans share Earth with many different **species** of animals and plants. All members of a species have one main purpose: to survive and produce offspring.

Survival and Adaptation

In every **ecosystem**, animals and plants compete with each other for resources, such as food, water, and sunlight. Each species has **characteristics** that give it advantages over other species and help it survive. These characteristics may help it hide from **predators**, survive extreme temperatures, trap its **prey**, or perhaps live for a long time without food or water.

Individual animals and plants that survive and produce offspring pass on their successful characteristics through their **genes**. If an environment or ecosystem changes, the characteristics that are needed to survive might change, too. Over time, this causes changes in a species. This is called adaptation.

▼ Spotted hyenas have extremely strong jaws and a powerful bite. This characteristic helps them kill their prey quickly.

The Scientists Behind the Science
Different types of scientists study animals, plants, and how they survive.
Scientist and Area of Study
Biologist Living things and their environments
Botanist Plants
Entomologist Insects
Mammalogist Mammals
Marine Biologist Marine life
Zoologist Animals

Word Watch

characteristics features or qualities of a living thing, such as having a long neck

ecosystem system of living and non-living things in an environment

genes part of cells that decide a living thing's characteristics and which are passed on to the next generation

predators animals that hunt and eat other animals

prey animals hunted or caught for food

species groups of living things that share the same characteristics and can breed with each other

If Cheetahs Are One of the Fastest Animals on Earth, Why Are They Endangered?

The cheetah is one of the fastest animals in the world, so it should be able to out-run any **predators**. The cheetah is, however, an **endangered species**. This is due to several reasons, including human activities such as hunting.

Habitat Destruction

Humans have cleared a lot of the land that is the natural **habitat** for cheetahs. Cheetahs live in open grassland habitats. Some cheetahs live in dry woodlands, **savanna**, or desert.

Humans have cleared the land to plant crops and raise grazing animals for food. The **prey** that cheetahs rely on for food, such as gazelles and hares, has moved elsewhere. Some cheetahs have been forced to attack grazing livestock for food. Attacking livestock puts them in danger of being shot by humans.

Sprinters, Not Marathon Runners!
Cheetahs can only maintain their speed for short distances. If they do not catch their prey within 550 yards (500 meters), they have to give up the chase.

Word Watch

endangered seriously at risk of extinction, or dying out

habitat home or environment of an animal or other living thing

predators animals that hunt and eat other animals

prey animals hunted or caught for food

savanna grassy plains with few trees

species groups of living things that share the same characteristics and can breed with each other

▲ A cheetah's speed helps it hunt its prey, but habitat destruction means there is less prey to hunt.

Hunted For Their Hides

When cheetahs have to move to unfamiliar environments due to land clearing, they become more **vulnerable** to hunters. Humans do not just kill cheetahs to protect their livestock. Some people trap and hunt cheetahs because they think it is sport. Other people hunt cheetahs so they can sell their spotted **hides**.

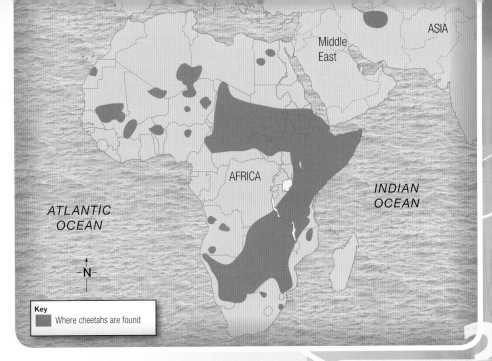

▲ One hundred years ago, there were an estimated 100,000 wild cheetahs in Africa and Asia. Today, there are only about 7,500 adult cheetahs. Most are found in Africa, except for about 60 to 100 that survive in northern Iran, in the Middle East.

▲ Hunters wear leopard and cheetah hides during a ceremony in Ethiopia.

Fast Animals

Animals that move at great speeds use their speed in two ways: as predators chasing prey and also to escape from predators that are chasing them.

The Fastest Animals

Area	Animal	Fastest Speed: Miles (Kilometers) Per Hour
On land	Cheetah	71 (114)
In water	Sailfish	70 (112)
In the air	Spine-tailed swift	106 (171)

Word Watch

hides skins of animals
vulnerable in danger of attack or harm

Cubs in Danger

While adult cheetahs are able to outsprint predators, such as lions and hyenas, their cubs are not as fast. While adult cheetahs are hunting prey, their cubs are often left unprotected and are vulnerable to attack. Cheetah numbers are declining in the wild and the species cannot afford to lose young cubs in this way.

Web Watch ▼

www.defenders.org/wildlife_and_
habitat/wildlife/cheetah.php
bigfive.jl.co.za/nat_cheetah_
management.htm

Why Do Chameleons Change Color?

Chameleons change color for many reasons. They may change color to **camouflage** themselves, to protect themselves from heat, or as a social signal to other chameleons. Some chameleons turn black when they are angry!

Changing Color

Chameleons change color so they can:

⮕ blend in with their surroundings and hide from hungry **predators**

⮕ protect themselves from excessive heat or attract more heat

⮕ assert their dominance, or show themselves as strong, within a group of chameleons

⮕ reveal the type of mood they are in

Chameleons change the color of their skin by altering the makeup of the **pigments** in their color-giving **cells**. They do this by releasing **hormones** into their blood. This can take either seconds or several minutes.

Where Are Chameleons Found?

There are about 150 species of chameleons around the world. Most species are found in Africa, Madagascar, India, Sri Lanka, and southern Europe.

Word Watch

camouflage hide or disguise oneself by blending in with the environment

cells basic building block of all living things, made up of chemicals and water

hormones substances produced by glands, which travel through the bloodstream to produce an effect on other organs and tissues

pigments substances used as coloring

predators animals that hunt and eat other animals

species groups of living things that share the same characteristics and can breed with each other

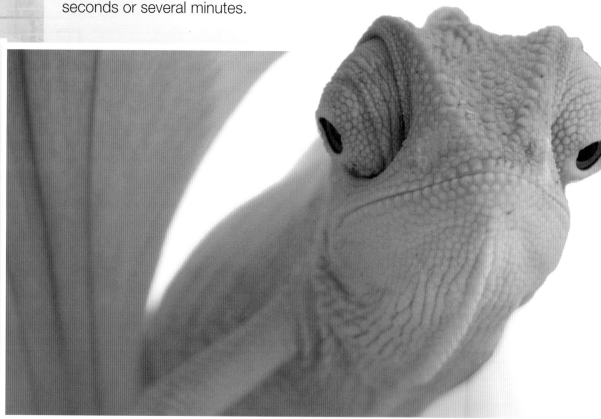

▲ A chameleon changes color so that it does not stand out against its background. This helps it hide from predators. Most chameleons are only able to change the green–brown levels of their skin, not change their color completely. Other **species** can change to and from pink, blue, red, orange, black, and yellow.

Other Survival Features

Apart from their ability to change color, chameleons also have other survival features. These features help them spot and escape from predators, such as birds and snakes, and also spot and catch their **prey**, such as insects and small lizards. These characteristics are:

- ➲ a flattened body shape that helps them quickly climb up trees
- ➲ a long tail that can be used for balance and as a weapon
- ➲ eyes that work independently of each other, so they can look in two different directions at once
- ➲ an extremely long tongue, which makes it easy to catch prey

Camouflage For Survival
Other animals that use camouflage to survive are stick insects, leopards, polar bears, Arctic owls, and bark bugs.

▲ A chameleon catches an insect with its long tongue.

Word Watch

prey animals hunted or caught for food

Web Watch ▼

www.chameleonsonline.com/
news.nationalgeographic.com/
news/2005/09/0926_050926_
chameleon.html

9

Which Creatures Can Survive at the Bottom of the Ocean?

Animals need sunlight and food to survive—yet some creatures have been discovered 20,000 feet (6,000 m) below sea level, where there is no sunlight, little food, and it is extremely cold.

Surviving The Deep-sea Environment

To survive in their extreme environment, deep-sea creatures have adapted in many ways. At about 3,300 feet (1,000 m) below sea level, the ocean becomes almost completely dark and no plants grow. Deep-sea creatures have different features or behaviors that allow them to survive here.

▲ A fish swims past giant tube worms on the ocean floor. Tube worms are able to survive the cold deep-sea environment by living near heat sources called hydrothermal vents.

Survival Features

Most deep-sea creatures move extremely slowly. There is very little food available to them and they have to conserve their energy. Many do not move at all and just wait for food to fall down to them from the upper layers of the ocean.

Because there is no sunlight at the bottom of the ocean, many of the creatures, such as anglerfish, have a cell in their bodies that produces light so they are able to catch their **prey**. Some deep-sea animals, such as tripod fish, use other senses to "see" in the darkness.

Animals such as giant tube worms move toward deep-sea vents to escape the cold temperatures. Vents are cracks in the ocean floor through which heat from deep within Earth escapes.

Word Watch

prey animals hunted or caught for food

Tripod Fish

Tripod fish rest on the ocean floor on long, thin extensions that come out from their three fins. These extensions help them ambush prey swimming or crawling beneath them. Long antennae help tripod fish locate their prey in the darkness.

Gulper Eel

An enormous mouth gives the gulper eel the best possible chance to catch the small amount of food that swims past it. It also has a stomach that stretches like elastic, so it can swallow creatures bigger than itself.

Anglerfish

The anglerfish catches its prey in the same way that an **angler** catches fish. It has a long growth that sticks out from its head and gives out light. This light acts as bait to attract prey.

Giant Tube Worms

The giant tube worm has no opening through which it feeds. Instead, it **absorbs** chemicals, such as oxygen and carbon dioxide, from hot vents. **Bacteria** that live inside the worm turn these chemicals into food.

▲ The anglerfish has a huge mouth and stomach. It can swallow prey up to two times its size.

Web Watch ▼

venturedeepocean.
org/life/

How Do Animals and Plants Survive in Deserts?

Animals and plants that live in deserts have to deal with long periods with extreme temperatures and without water. They have developed clever ways to survive the harsh conditions.

Surviving With Very Little Water

Desert animals and plants live in areas with little water. Deserts receive very little **precipitation** and many deserts do not have rain for long periods of time. Often, when it does rain, it rains heavily and there are floods. One source of water is dew, the tiny drops of moisture that form on cool surfaces at night.

Collecting and Storing Water

Desert animals and plants collect and store water in different ways. Some animals, such as the water-holding frog, store water in their bodies. Some plants store water in their leaves, stems, or roots. Some also have waxy leaves that stop water **evaporating**.

The fog-basking beetle collects dew in a surprising way. It stands on its head so that dew that forms during foggy weather collects on its body and trickles down to its mouth. The thorny devil also collects dew. Some animals get the water they need from food sources, such as plants and the **carcasses** of other animals. Cacti are a particularly useful source of water for insects.

▼ Lithops are a pair of leaves that are able to keep moisture within them. They look so much like stones, they are also known as "living stones."

▲ The water-holding frog stores water in its body. During dry spells, it replaces its skin with a cocoon wrapping that acts like a plastic bag, keeping water inside the frog.

grooves to catch water

▶ The thorny devil has a clever way of gathering water. The grooves in its body lead to its mouth, so any dew that collects in the grooves is not wasted.

Surviving Extreme Temperatures

Desert animals and plants have had to adapt to extreme temperatures. Deserts can be hot, like the Sahara, or cold, like polar deserts. Some deserts have extremes of both hot and cold temperatures.

Some animals survive by staying away from the heat. They may be **nocturnal** or they may burrow under the ground, like the golden mole. Some animals have physical features that help them cool down, such as jackrabbits and fennec foxes, which use their large ears to release heat. Some plants have silver leaves, which help **reflect** the sun's rays, keeping the plant cooler.

Spreading Seeds

Some desert plants form tumbleweeds, where part of the plant above the ground breaks off and tumbles away. Tumbleweeds have hundreds of thousands of seeds inside them. As they tumble away, they drop and spread their seeds. Some of the seeds will survive and grow, spreading the desert plant.

▲ A fennec fox has very large ears through which heat escapes, keeping its body cool.

◄ A golden mole burrows just under the surface of the sand to keep cool.

Word Watch

nocturnal active at night

reflect return or bounce back

Web Watch ▼

www.desertusa.com/survive.html

13

What Is a Parasite?

A parasite is an **organism** that lives in or on another organism, called a host, and depends on that organism for survival. A parasite might get its **nutrients** from the host or it might use the host as a place to raise its young.

A One-way Relationship

In a parasitic relationship, the benefits are all one way. The parasite receives the nutrients or environment that it requires. The host receives no benefits at all. In most cases, the host is harmed in some way.

Endoparasites

Parasites that live inside their hosts are called endoparasites. Examples of endoparasites are tapeworms and hookworms. They live in the intestines of their hosts. Hookworms often find their way inside humans, usually through the skin. If not treated, hookworms can cause severe malnutrition and even death.

Parasites On Parasites!
Some parasites live off other parasites. These are known as epiparasites.

▼ Tapeworms are endoparasites that infect humans and other animals.

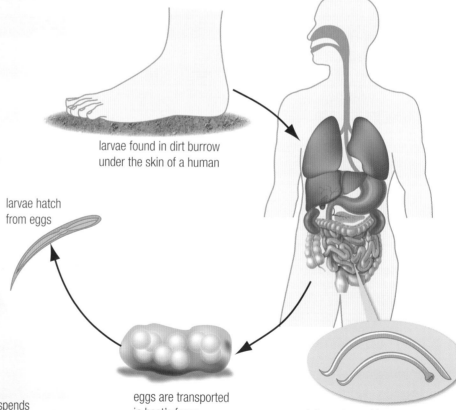

larvae found in dirt burrow under the skin of a human

larvae hatch from eggs

▶ A hookworm spends its adult life inside a host.

eggs are transported in host's feces

adults mate and lay eggs in the small intestine of the host

Ectoparasites

Parasites that live on their hosts are called ectoparasites. Examples of ectoparasites are leeches, lice, mites, and fleas. Ectoparasites move from host to host to find better nourishment or once they have used up the supply from a host.

Many ectoparasites live off the blood of their host. They can transmit deadly diseases into a host's blood system.

▲ A flea pierces the skin of a host and sucks its blood. The most obvious sign of the presence of fleas is the host's itchiness.

Parasitic Plants

Parasites also exist in the plant world. Examples are mistletoe and dodder. Dodder is a spindly yellow plant that wraps itself around other plants, stealing their water and nutrients.

▶ Mistletoe attaches itself to trees and shrubs and uses its roots to steal nutrients away from the host.

Mutualism

When two organisms form a relationship where both receive benefits, it is known as mutualism. An example is the relationship between cleaner shrimps and fish. Cleaner shrimps remove parasites and food from the teeth of the fish, and the fish gets clean, healthy teeth.

Moving from Host to Host

A flea cannot fly but it is able to jump 100 times its own body length.

Web Watch ▼

www.wisegeek.com/what-is-a-parasite.htm

What Happens When a Food Chain Breaks?

When one of the living things in a food chain becomes **extinct** or leaves an **ecosystem**, it breaks the chain. The living things above it in the chain need to find a new source of energy or they will die out. The living things below it in the chain have a greater chance of survival because one of their predators is no longer around.

Food Chains

Living things within an ecosystem depend on each other for energy, in the form of food and **nutrients**. This is known as a food chain.

In Water and On Land

Food chains exist both in water and on land. In the ocean, sea plants and **plankton** are eaten by small fish, which are eaten by bigger fish, which are eaten by even bigger fish, which are eaten by humans and some other land animals.

Herbivores and Carnivores

Herbivores pass on far less energy to the next link on the food chain than carnivores. This is because they use most of their energy in their daily activities, rather than storing it in their bodies.

Word watch

bacteria single-celled microorganisms

ecosystem system of living and non-living things in an environment

extinct no longer existing as a species

fungi toadstools and mushrooms

nutrients things that provide energy for growth

photosynthesis process by which plants produce food using energy from the sun, water, and carbon dioxide

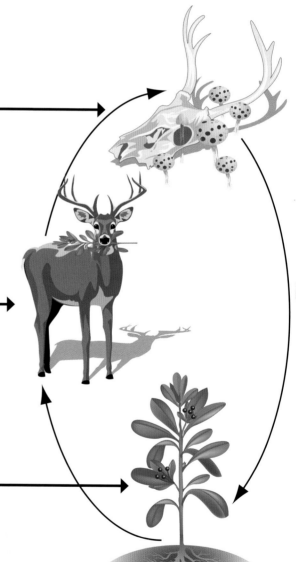

3 »
Finally, there are the decomposers. These are **fungi** and **bacteria** that live off the dead consumers. Decomposers return nutrients to the ground, which the primary producers then use, starting the process all over again.

2 »
Next in the chain are the consumers. These are animals and a few plants that cannot make their own food and need to find it elsewhere. There may be several consumers in a single food chain.

1 »
At the bottom of a food chain are the primary producers. These plants produce their own food through **photosynthesis**.

« 4
The cycle continues.

Food Pyramids

In reality, a food chain is more like a pyramid. From the bottom up, there are fewer and fewer consumers on each level of the pyramid. This is because the amount of energy that is transferred gets smaller and smaller the farther along the food chain it goes. In most food chains, the amount of energy is only enough to support four or five links or four or five types of living thing.

few merlins

some blackbirds

many beetle larvae

many roots

▲ There are more consumers on lower levels of the food pyramid and less on higher levels.

Consumers

There are three types of consumers:

➲ herbivores, which eat only plants
➲ carnivores, which eat only animals
➲ omnivores, which eat plants and animals

Food Webs

Most animals are part of more than one food chain, because they eat more than one type of **prey**. Most food chains are part of a larger food web.

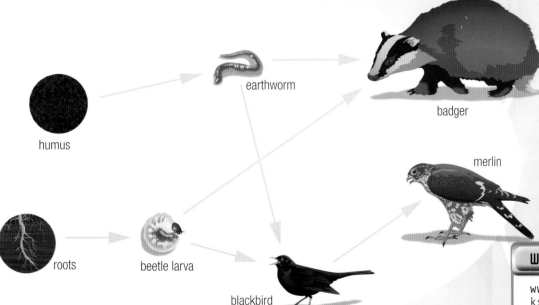

humus

earthworm

badger

merlin

roots

beetle larva

blackbird

▲ There are many food chains within the one food web.

Word Watch

plankton tiny, free-floating sea creatures

prey animals hunted or caught for food

Web Watch ▼

www.bbc.co.uk/schools/ks2bitesize/science/activities/food_chains.shtml

www.vtaide.com/png/foodchains.htm

What Does "Survival of the Fittest" Mean?

"Survival of the fittest" is often used to describe one of Charles Darwin's **theories**. His theory is that within a **species**, there are some individuals that possess **characteristics** suited to their environment. These individuals are more likely to survive and pass these characteristics on to their offspring. This is part of the theory of **evolution**.

The Voyage of the *Beagle*

Charles Darwin (1809–1882) was a British **naturalist** who sailed on the voyage of HMS *Beagle* between 1831 and 1836. The voyage took Darwin around the world. He collected plant and animal **specimens** and observed wildlife in its natural **habitats** at all the locations he visited.

Charles Darwin

Charles Darwin was born in Shrewsbury, England, in 1809. Both his father and grandfather were doctors. Darwin also studied medicine, but his heart was elsewhere. His passion for collecting beetles led to a career in science. Following his voyage on HMS *Beagle*, he developed his theories about evolution.

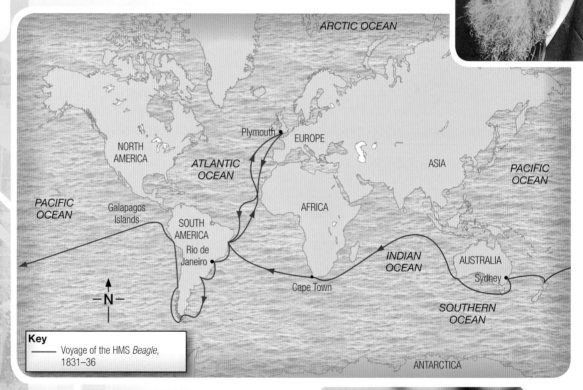

▲ Darwin visited many parts of the world on the voyage of the HMS *Beagle*.

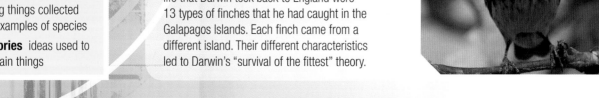

▶ Among the specimens of plant and animal life that Darwin took back to England were 13 types of finches that he had caught in the Galapagos Islands. Each finch came from a different island. Their different characteristics led to Darwin's "survival of the fittest" theory.

The Galapagos Finches

Darwin noticed that each type of finch specimen he had collected in the Galapagos Islands had characteristics that seemed to fit the environment of its island. On islands that had many seeds, the finches had beaks that were good for splitting seeds. On islands that had lots of insects, the finches had beaks that were good for catching insects. Yet the different types of finches were also similar in many ways.

The Theory of Natural Selection

Darwin's **observations** led to him develop his theory of "natural selection," which is sometimes referred to as "survival of the fittest." According to Darwin, the living things best suited to their environment are more likely to reach breeding age. As a result, the characteristics that have helped them survive are passed on to their offspring in their **genes**. Over several generations, in different environments, species that were once very similar can appear quite different to each other.

▲ More dark-colored peppered moths than light-colored peppered moths survived when the tree trunks looked a darker color.

An Example: the English Peppered Moth

Before the **Industrial Revolution**, the trees where peppered moths lived were covered in light-colored **lichen**. Light-colored moths were **camouflaged**, while dark-colored moths were easily picked off by birds, so there were far more light-colored moths. The many factories of the Industrial Revolution produced soot that killed lichen. The dark-colored moths were camouflaged against the dark trees and became more numerous, and the light-colored ones were eaten by the birds.

Word Watch

camouflaged hidden or disguised by blending in with the environment

genes part of cells that decide a living thing's characteristics and which are passed on to its offspring

Industrial Revolution time in the 1800s when machines were introduced and large factories were set up

lichen type of fungus

observations information that is gained by watching something carefully

Why Do Giraffes Have Such Long Necks?

For a long time, it was believed that giraffes have long necks so that they can eat leaves from tall trees. Another **theory** was that long necks helped them watch out for **predators**. Recent scientific research, however, suggests their long necks are linked to their mating habits.

Only Seven Vertebrae

Even though giraffes have very long necks, they have only seven **vertebrae** in their necks. This is the same as most mammals, including humans. The difference in a giraffe's neck is that its vertebrae are stretched to produce its long neck.

To Help Them Reach Leaves in Tall Trees?

Although it might seem obvious that giraffes have long necks to help them reach leaves growing too high for other animals, there is a lot of evidence to suggest this theory is false. When giraffes feed, they mostly keep their necks **horizontal**. Even in the dry season, when food is hard to find, they still prefer to find leaves on low bushes rather than turn their attention upward. Only in the rainy season, when leaves are plentiful, do they eat from tall trees rather than bushes.

To Watch Out for Predators?

Giraffes do use their height advantage to scan their surroundings for potential predators, but they have other successful defensive features, too. They are very fast and they can run up to 37 miles (60 km) per hour. They also have a very powerful kick that can kill predators instantly.

◀ The evidence does not support the theory that giraffes have long necks so they can reach leaves from tall trees.

▼ Giraffes have many defensive features, such as running, so their long necks are not essential for escaping predators.

▲ A bull's neck can weigh up to 130 pounds (90 kilograms) and stretch more than 6 feet (1.8 m), so the force when two bulls fight is extreme.

To Fight for Dominance?

The most likely explanation for a giraffe's long neck is that it **evolved** through the mating habits of the male giraffe. Male giraffes, called bulls, fight each other using their necks. The winner gets to mate with the female giraffes.

When two competing bulls first face each other, they point their noses upward to try to outdo each other. If there is an obvious height difference, the smaller bull will often run away.

If a fight does occur, the bulls swing their necks and heads and collide with great force. The bulls with the longest necks usually win, and this **characteristic** is passed down to their offspring in their **genes**. Over millions of years, this has resulted in the necks of giraffes getting longer and stronger (see the theory of natural selection on pages 18–19).

(see the theory of natural selection on pages 18–19).

Mating Habits

Many animals have certain habits or displays that they must perform before mating. Male peacocks display their plumage to compete for the affections of peahens. Rams butt heads to compete for the chance to mate with female goats.

Longest Animal

Despite growing to almost 20 feet (6 m) from the tip of its tail to the top of its head, the giraffe is not the longest animal on Earth. The reticulated python, which can stretch for more than 33 feet (10 m), is the longest. Some **species** of tapeworm can also stretch up to 33 feet (10 m) long.

Word Watch

characteristic feature or quality of a living thing, such as having a long neck

evolved gradually changed and developed

genes part of cells that decide a living thing's characteristics and which are passed on to its offspring

species groups of living things that share the same characteristics and can breed with each other

Web Watch ▼

www.kidsplanet.org/
factsheets/giraffe.html
www.how-come.net/
giraffeneck.html

Which Animals Migrate the Farthest?

Animals usually **migrate** to search for food or to escape extreme weather conditions. Animals migrate on land, in the oceans, and in the air. The exact distance that particular **species** travel is difficult to track, but the sooty shearwater is believed to migrate the farthest.

Migration by Flight

The longest recorded annual migration by a bird is 40,400 miles (65,000 km) by the sooty shearwater. Another bird that undertakes a long migratory journey is the arctic tern. The arctic tern may have a longer migration route than the sooty shearwater, but it has never been tracked to check the distance it actually covers in the air. The arctic tern travels between the Arctic and Antarctic each year.

Solo Migration

The longest recorded migration by an individual reptile was more than 12,500 miles (20,000 km) by a leatherback turtle. The turtle swam from Indonesia, across the Pacific Ocean to Oregon, on the United States northwestern coast, then back to Indonesia.

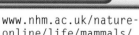

Web Watch ▼

www.nhm.ac.uk/nature-online/life/mammals/migration/index.html

news.nationalgeographic.com/news/2006/08/060808-bird-migration.html

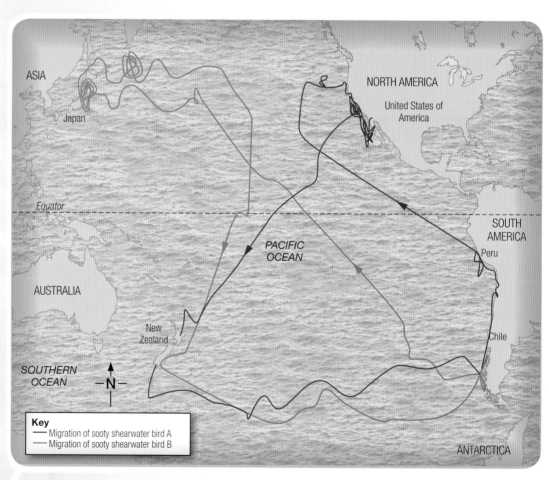

▲ Each year, the sooty shearwater flies from the northern hemisphere to breed on Pacific islands in the southern hemisphere. The 40,400-mile (65,000-km) distance reflects their actual flying distance, not the direct route from the western coast of the United States to New Zealand. The birds fly in a wide figure-eight pattern across the Pacific, so their flight is longer. This map shows the flights of two different sooty shearwater birds.

Migration on Land

The largest land migration involves more than 2 million animals. In November each year, the **herbivores** of the Serengeti begin moving south to where wet weather has made the grassland rich in **nutrients**. From December until March, they remain in the south and give birth to their young. As the dry weather approaches and the grassland in the south begins to dry out, the animals start moving off and follow the rains back north.

▲ Each year, thousands of caribou walk across the Arctic tundra between their summer and winter ranges. Some of them cover more than 1,850 miles (3,000 km) in their round trip across this vast, flat, treeless area.

Word Watch

herbivores animals that only eat plants

nutrients things that provide energy for growth

▶ The Serengeti is an area in Africa that extends from northwestern Tanzania to southwestern Kenya. Herbivores of the Serengeti, such as zebras and wildebeest, make a yearly migration, following the rain.

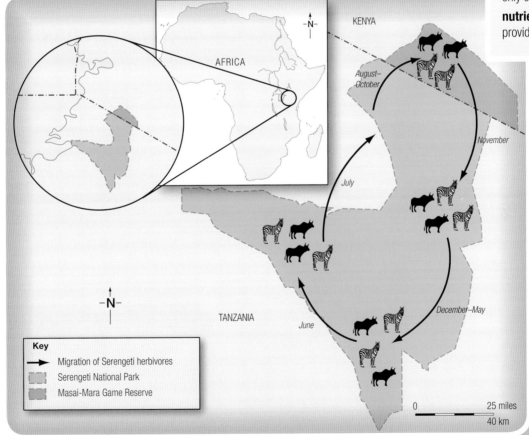

KENYA

AFRICA

August–October

November

July

June

TANZANIA

December–May

Key

→ Migration of Serengeti herbivores

▢ Serengeti National Park

▢ Masai-Mara Game Reserve

0   25 miles
         40 km

Migration at Sea

Some humpback whales travel from the Antarctic to the northern oceans each year in search of warm water to raise their young. Some make a round trip of more than 5,000 miles (8,000 km), which is the longest yearly migration by any mammal.

Web Watch ▼

www.tanzaniaparks.com/serengeti.html

Do Any Plants Eat Animals?

More than 600 **species** of plants eat animals. These plants are called **carnivorous** plants. Carnivorous plants usually grow in soil that is low in **nutrients**. They need to get their nutritional requirements some other way, so they catch and eat animals.

Word Watch

carnivorous meat-eating

nutrients things that provide energy for growth

photosynthesis process by which plants produce food using energy from the sun, water, and carbon dioxide

prey animals hunted or caught for food

species groups of living things that share the same characteristics and can breed with each other

Producers or Consumers?

The fact that some plants eat meat raises the question: are these plants producers or consumers in a food chain (see page 16)? Carnivorous plants are actually both. They are able to produce energy through **photosynthesis**, so they are considered producers, but they are also consumers because they depend on other living things for most of their nutrients.

Insect-eaters

Plants that eat animals usually eat insects. Different plants trap their **prey** in different ways. They might have sticky leaves, such as the butterwort plant, or rolled leaves that act as a trap, with waxy, slippery surfaces. Some plants, such as the Venus flytrap, have leaves that snap shut and trap insects inside.

▲ Pitcher plants have long, deep cavities that insects fall into. The insects cannot climb out because of slippery leaves or thorns that block their way.

▶ Several species of butterwort trap insects on their sticky leaves. The insects cannot crawl or fly away.

Web Watch ▼

www.sarracenia.com/
faq/faq2000.html

How the Venus Flytrap Catches Insects

Most Venus flytraps grow in bogs where there is a lack of the chemical nitrogen in the soil. They catch passing insects, which provide them with the nutrients they cannot get out of the ground.

American Flytraps

Venus flytraps have been introduced to various locations around the world. They originally came from the states of North Carolina and South Carolina in the United States.

1 »

Attracting an Insect

Glands on the inside of the Venus flytrap produce a sweet-smelling **nectar** that attracts insects. On the inside of the leaf are hairs called trigger hairs.

2 »

Trapping the Insect

When an insect walks across the leaf and touches the trigger hairs, the trap closes. Small insects have a chance to escape though the narrow openings in the trap, because Venus flytraps do not want to waste their time with small insects. If the trap has caught a large insect, the plant can sense it struggling and tightens the trap shut.

3 »

Eating the Insect

The Venus flytrap releases juices that help digest the soft body parts of the insect. After a few days, the trap reopens and the hard skeleton of the insect is blown away in the wind.

trigger hairs

cricket caught inside trap

Word Watch

nectar sugary liquid produced by flowers

25

Do Plants Grow on the Dark Floor of a Rain Forest?

The floor of a rain forest gets so little sunlight that no small plants are able to survive there. Larger plants, such as trees and ferns, can reach up to sunlight in upper layers of the rain forest. Other living things, however, do grow and survive on the dark ground.

The Layers of a Rain Forest

The heavy rain that falls in a rain forest constantly drips down to the lower levels, but sunlight is blocked out and not a lot penetrates to the rain forest floor. Plants need sunlight so that they can produce their food through **photosynthesis**. The only parts of plants seen on the floor of a rain forest are the bottom of the trunks of trees, which get their sunlight in the upper layers of the rain forest.

What Is a Rain Forest?

Rain forest is thick forest that has annual rainfall of 80 inches (200 cm) or more. Many rain forests are located in tropical regions, near the equator.

Word Watch

fungi toadstools and mushrooms

photosynthesis process by which plants produce food using energy from the sun, water, and carbon dioxide

species groups of living things that share the same characteristics and can breed with each other

Emergent Layer

The emergent layer is made up of the tops of the tallest trees. Some rain forests' trees stand more than 200 feet (60 m) tall. Among the animal life in this layer are birds, bats, and some insect **species**.

Canopy

The canopy acts as a roof over the bottom two layers. The leaves and branches of the trees intertwine, providing homes for birds and climbing, swinging animals. Some plants take root in the branches of the trees.

Understorey

The plants in the understorey have large leaves to help catch whatever sunlight makes it through the canopy. Insect and animal life thrive in the damp, dark reaches of the understorey.

Forest Floor

The forest floor receives less than 2 percent of the sunlight that hits the tops of the trees in the emergent layer. No small plants grow on the floor of a rain forest, but **fungi** are a very common feature.

Fungi and Dead Leaves

Fungi are found on the rain forest floor. They are different from plants in that they do not photosynthesize. Instead, they feed on **decomposing** plant and animal life.

Dead leaves and ferns also cover the rain forest floor. These things, as well as the fungi when they die off, provide the soil with **nutrients** that help the trees grow. The floor of a rain forest is so **humid** that leaves completely decompose in just a few days, rather than the few weeks it takes in less humid areas.

▲ Fungi feed on plant litter and animal remains on the rain forest floor.

Word Watch

decomposing rotting or wasting away

humid containing lots of water vapor in the air

nutrients things that provide energy for growth

Web Watch ▼

www.srl.caltech.edu/ personnel/krubal/ rainforest/Edit560s6/ www/whlayers.html

www.rainforestanimals. net/rainforest.html

Why Do Bears Hibernate?

Hibernation is when an animal shuts down its body during winter. Bears hibernate during the winter because this is a time when their food supplies drop dramatically. By hibernating, bears are able to get through the winter without starving.

What Happens to a Bear's Body When It Hibernates?

Hibernating is different to sleeping. Bears sometimes wake up and move around in the winter, and they also remain in a state where they can react if in danger from a **predator**. The biggest changes in a hibernating bear's body are its reduced heartbeat, which is much slower than normal, and the small drop in its body temperature.

Other Changes

Bears do not need to go to the toilet while they are hibernating. Other hibernating animals have to wake up and get rid of their waste from time to time or they would be poisoned, but bears have a way of recycling their waste while they are hibernating.

How Long Does a Bear Hibernate?

The length of hibernation depends on the **species** of bear and the location of its habitat. Some bears can hibernate for up to seven months.

Web Watch ▼

www.pbs.org/wgbh/
nova/satoyama/
hibernation.html

▲ Pregnant female bears still give birth to their cubs even when hibernating. They do not take in extra food while they are hibernating, but they make sure they have enough fat on them to produce milk for their cubs.

Preparing for Hibernation

Bears do not just crawl into a cave and hibernate when it starts snowing. They prepare for hibernation for the entire time between hibernations. When they hibernate, their body still requires a source of energy to continue to function. There is no source of energy available to them during hibernation, so they have to store enough energy, in the form of fat, before winter. Between hibernations, they eat as much as possible.

Finding a Shelter

Once its body is ready for hibernation, a bear has to find a suitable location to hibernate. Caves and hollow tree logs are popular because they provide the bear with some security from predators.

The shelter has to be positioned so that warm weather is unlikely to be noticed. The bear does not want its body to think that the winter is over too soon. If it finished its hibernation early, there would be no **prey** for it to survive on.

Other Hibernating Animals
Other animals that hibernate are some species of:
➲ squirrels
➲ hedgehogs
➲ bats
➲ snakes

▶ During the warmer months, a bear prepares for hibernation by eating as much as possible.

Word Watch

prey animals hunted or caught for food

Web Watch ▼

www.essortment.com/all/whybearshibern_rnnm.htm

What Are the Most Intelligent Animals After Humans?

Brain size is a good clue to the intelligence of animals. Chimpanzees and other apes top the list when it comes to determining the most intelligent animals after humans.

Studying Animal Intelligence

When studying animal intelligence, scientists make **observations** and do tests in particular areas. They measure an animal's ability to:

- ➲ shape and use tools to find food and to use as weapons
- ➲ solve a range of problems without training
- ➲ use its memory to help it catch food
- ➲ learn language, such as recognizing and learning signs that are taught to it
- ➲ display emotions

Brain Size

The bigger the brain, the more options an animal has to undertake tasks. Different parts of the brain serve different functions. Like humans, chimpanzees have large areas of the brain for learning, memory, and decision-making.

Jane Goodall

Jane Goodall (1934–) is a British **primatologist** who has been studying the chimpanzees of Tanzania since 1960. Goodall also campaigns for the protection of chimpanzees and other primates. In 1977, she established the Jane Goodall Institute for Wildlife Research, Education, and Conservation, which supports research on chimpanzees in the wild.

Word Watch

observations
information that is gained by watching something carefully

primatologist
someone who studies apes, monkeys, and other primates

Web Watch ▼

animals.
nationalgeographic.
com/animals/mammals/
chimpanzee.html
www.janegoodall.org

▲ Jane Goodall studies the behavior of chimpanzees in Tanzania, learning how they live and behave.

Chimpanzees

There is evidence of the intelligence of chimpanzees in the way that they use tools and go about tasks. Their intelligence is not surprising, because chimpanzees are the animals that are most closely related to humans. Other **species** of ape also rank highly in the area of animal intelligence.

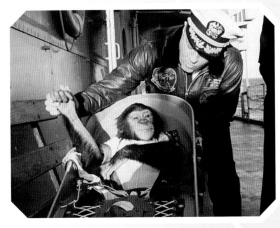

▲ The chimpanzee Ham was sent into space due to his intelligence and his ability to follow instructions.

▲ Chimpanzees can make a sponge out of a wad of leaves to soak up rainwater and then squeeze the water into their mouths.

▲ Chimpanzees use stones and logs as tools to crack nuts.

▲ Chimpanzees are able to learn and use human sign language.

▲ Chimpanzees can shape sticks and grass stems to dig for food.

Word Watch

species groups of living things that share the same characteristics and can breed with each other

Index